A PASSION FOR PURITY

A PASSION FOR PURITY
Protecting God's Precious
Gift of Virginity

by

Carla A. Stephens

Harrison House
Tulsa, Oklahoma

06 05 04 03   10 9 8 7 6 5 4 3 2 1

A Passion for Purity—
Protecting God's Precious Gift of Virginity
ISBN 1-57794-568-9
Copyright © 2003 by Carla A. Stephens
P.O. Box 1630
Fayetteville, GA 30214

Published by Harrison House, Inc.
P.O. Box 35035
Tulsa, Oklahoma 74153

Dedication

I dedicate this book to my loving husband:
To Jesse who continues to be a wonderful, loving,
and kind husband. I thank God for you every day.
You mean the world to me.

To My Parents:

In memory of the late Sam and Evelyn Owens.
Thank you for believing in me.
I love you and miss you both very much.

To My Spiritual Parents:

Pastors Creflo and Taffi Dollar.

It is because of you that I am able to write this book.

Thank you so much for teaching me
the truth in God's Word.

I love you both, and I thank God for birthing me
into such an anointed family.

To My Sisters and Brothers:

Rhonda, Tammy, Rodney, Alicia, and Caron,
I love you all.

May this book serve as a resource as you raise
your beautiful sons and daughters.

Foreword

In these pages you will find a true picture of purity. This book explores the topic of virginity and brings it down to a relatable and understandable subject. *A Passion for Purity* shows you how abstaining from sex is accepting a gift from God. It emphasizes how those who choose to practice purity are also protecting a treasure from God.

A Passion for Purity is a must read for any young person, parent, or minister. Carla Stephens has written a book that will be a blessing to you as you seek out a purpose for remaining pure. She is a woman of God who continues to hold young people accountable to the things of God. I admire her compassion and commitment to seeing young people walk in purity. As the youth pastor of World Changers Church International, pastored by Dr. Creflo A. Dollar, I have invited her to minister on several occasions. Each time she ministers students leave with not only a good message, but with the wisdom on how to live their lives pleasing to God. Her experience with young ladies and her understanding of the Word of God have more than qualified her to write on such a prominent subject as purity.

As I travel across this nation and around the world, I have found that this generation is in need of encouragement to live by the Word of God. Never before have morals been ignored as much as they are today. There is an imminent need for each one of us to take a stand for what is right in the eyes of God. This book will do just that—encourage each young person to make a quality decision to remain pure before God.

In each chapter, Carla gets right to the point—painting a picture of how to maintain your innocence. She shows you the necessary things needed in order to boldly resist the temptation of sexual immorality. If you are open to learning the truth, you can apply these values to find the purpose of God for your life.

Decisions. That is what purity is about. That is what this book is about. A lifestyle of purity starts in the heart. You must support it with your decisions. I believe that we must all avoid the trap of having sex before marriage. A relationship without purity is a relationship headed for sin and possibly destruction. It is your values in God that should guide your choices in relationships. Living a lifestyle of purity requires work and obedience to God; however, the rewards will far outweigh any sacrifices made. *A Passion for Purity* shows us that true purity flees from temptation, sin, and compromise.

The principles found here are both helpful and hopeful. This book serves as a help to those who have fallen in their quest for purity, and hope to those who continue to live pure and free from sexual sin. Both can experience a wonderful beginning to maintaining innocence. *A Passion for Purity* will usher you into God's presence and purpose for your life. It would serve you well to read this book over and over and study what you have read. Carla, I thank you for writing such a wonderful book and having a true passion for purity!

—Lee Wilson, Founder
Lee Wilson Ministries, Inc.

Contents

Introduction

Many women today are completely unaware of their true value. Most have a poor self-image and struggle daily with negative thoughts about themselves. Airbrushed images of the "ideal woman" are everywhere, giving false impressions of how we ought to dress, think, feel, and act. In our attempt to become what we see, we sacrifice something that God treasures dearly—our virginity—and end up feeling confused, depressed, hurt, and rejected by those around us.

Over the years, virginity has become a dirty word. Every day our senses are bombarded with reports that contradict what God's Word has to say about the sanctity of marriage and the purpose for sexual relationships. The same media that display the seemingly ideal woman with the ostensibly perfect proportions often portray relationships in which couples rush to the bedroom without much more than a "hello."

In this world, lust is often mistaken for love. However, it is possible to stay pure in an impure world. In fact, it is necessary that we do so in order to enjoy our lives to the fullest of God's plan.

Jeremiah 29:11 NIV says, "'For I know the plans I have for you,' declares the Lord, 'plans to prosper you and not to harm you, plans to give you hope and a future.'" God has a purpose for you, and He has set up specific tokens—walls of protection—to guard against anything that would keep you from experiencing the fullness of that purpose.

The tokens of virginity are purity, innocence, and the blood. These tokens act as barriers to negative outside influences that try to inhibit God's plan for your life—for prosperity, hope, and a bright future. These three tokens defend you from the enemy's attempts to steal the precious treasure of your virginity.

This treasure is often misunderstood or overlooked.

My prayer is that as you read on, you would gain better insight into the precious, valuable gift of your virginity. Even if you are no longer a virgin, you will discover that all things can be made new with God. It is never too late to discover the tokens of virginity and to discover a new passion for purity.

Chapter One

What's the Big Deal?

For this is the will of God, that you should be conse-
crated (separated and set apart for pure and holy living):
that you should abstain and shrink from all sexual vice,
that each one of you should know how to possess (control,
manage) his own body in consecration (purity, separated
from things profane) and honor, for God has not called us
to impurity but to consecration [to dedicate ourselves to
the most thorough purity].

1 THESSALONIANS 4:3,4,7 AMP

"Virginity: Teach your kids it's not a dirty word." I'll
never forget this billboard brightly painted in red. It was
like an oasis in the desert as I drove along the highway,
seeing so many ads arbitrarily linking physical pleasure
with different products.

Piquing customers' sexual appetite seems to be the standard mode of operation in popular media today. The highest-ranking movies, television programs, and music send messages that contradict biblical values by portraying virginity as an old-fashioned concept. Sadly, many around us seem to share this view on sexuality. Women who choose to remain virgins are considered "frigid" or "prudish." Unfortunately, to many the idea of saving sex for marriage is no longer desirable or realistic.

Virginity is, indeed, an old concept. In fact, it dates back to biblical times. God, the Creator Himself, who knows what is best for His creation, presented the concept of virginity to us. We didn't come up with the idea of abstaining from sex before marriage. God did it for our protection and to keep us in union with Him.

Why, then, does it appear that virginity is a faux pas in our popular culture? The problem lies in the fact that most people think virginity only involves the physical body. However, this is not at all the case. The apostle Paul told us in Romans 12:1 that keeping ourselves pure is our "spiritual act of worship" (NIV). Therefore, when one remains sexually pure, her body and spirit join together as one unit to worship God. Her physical act affects her spiritual act.

The acts of the human body will always affect the acts of the human spirit, and vice versa. Look at what happens, for instance, when a person accepts Jesus Christ as her personal Savior and becomes born again.* Her body is automatically transformed into the temple, or house, of the Holy Spirit. (1 Cor. 6:19.)

Contrary to what many people may think, the Holy Spirit does not live in a building or on a distant planet. Neither is He some "thing." The Holy Spirit is a person—the third Person of the Trinity—who lives inside of us in order to teach, guide, and direct us. (John 16:13.) He's the "hunch" or "feeling" we get when we know we're doing something wrong. In fact, the Holy Spirit helps us live pleasing lives before God.

---

* If you would like more information about making Jesus your Lord, please see the prayer of salvation at the end of this book.

Bought With a Price

In light of this fact, it is important that you realize you do not own your body anymore. You gave up your rights when you became born again. Paul reminds us of this in 1 Corinthians 6:19-20: "...ye are not your own...for ye are bought with a price: therefore glorify God in your body, and in your spirit, which are God's."

Jesus paid a high price to buy us back from the curse of sin and death. (Gal. 3:13.) When we accept Him as Lord and Savior, we are saying, "Jesus, I give up my right to control my life. Your blood paid the price for my sin, and I promise to serve, worship, and submit my will to You forever."

It is out of respect and gratitude for Jesus' sacrifice that we "...abstain and shrink from all sexual vice...know how to possess (control, manage) [our] own body in consecration (purity, separated from things profane) and honor, not [to be used] in the passion of lust like the heathen, who are ignorant of the true God and have no knowledge of His will" (1 Thess. 4:3-5 AMP). In other words, we cannot ignore God's ownership of us and do whatever we want to His house.

Think of it this way. Suppose you buy a house worth millions of dollars. You spend years negotiating the price, inspecting the property, and getting the money together. Finally the day arrives when you can move in. Over the next several weeks you paint, clean, and decorate your new home until you get it just the way you want it. You even have a security system installed for extra protection.

Every night you turn on the alarm, even though you live in a safe neighborhood and no one has ever broken into your home. However, one night you decide not to turn on the alarm because you'll only be gone for a few hours. You return a little while later to find your home vandalized and all your valuables taken.

Would you kick yourself for not turning on that alarm? I would!

This is not unlike what happens when you become a believer and the Holy Spirit makes His home in you. In the years before you met Jesus, you may have been gossiping, lying, stealing, cheating, having sex outside of marriage, drinking—in short, living the life of a sinner. Yet, even though you were unaware of it, God had been carefully orchestrating your salvation—sending His messengers your way, telling others to intercede on your behalf—so that eventually the day would come when you would accept Christ and the Holy Spirit would move in to live in your heart.

For a while you had your spiritual alarm set. In other words, you were alert to the voice of the Holy Spirit because you read the Word, prayed, resisted temptation, controlled your thoughts, and obeyed God wholeheartedly out of your newly discovered love for Jesus. However, the time came when you got tired of abstaining from worldly things, and you turned off your alarm. Before you realized what had happened, you allowed God's house to be vandalized. In other words, you gave in to temptation and sinned, and the treasure of your virginity was stolen.

Virginity is indeed a treasure, benefiting the virgin and his or her relationship with God. In 1 Corinthians 7:32-34, Paul states that a virgin is able to concentrate more on the things of God than on the distractions and temporary pleasures of the world. A virgin can focus one's attention on pleasing God, whereas a non-virgin must contend with the distraction of wanting to please a partner in bed.

This distraction is the natural result of awakening sexual desire. Think about it. If you'd never tasted chocolate ice cream, you would never crave it. Right? The same is true with sex. It's much more difficult to resist the urge to have sex once you've experienced it.

Therefore, virginity is its own defense mechanism. It is designed to help you combat the strong forces of sexual temptation and prevent you from having to reap the consequences associated with sex outside of marriage.

Contrary to what people may tell you, God's idea of virginity is not to keep you from having fun. God is not some "cosmic killjoy" ready to zap us when it looks like we might be having a good time. Not at all! His greatest desire is for us to have life—abundantly. (John 10:10.) God's purpose is not to steal our pleasure by making us cling to an outdated and undesirable thing called virginity.

Rather, virginity is His precious gift to us to be protected at all costs. When you hold on to your gift of virginity, it signifies that you have been set apart, consecrated, for God and the person He's created for you to marry.

It means that you have given thought to the future, weighed all of your options, and chosen to set yourself apart unto God.

Because you are consecrated unto God, He sees you in a special way. It can be loosely compared to the way you think about that favorite shirt in your closet. In your mind you have set that item aside from all the others because you think it's special. No one else can wear it but you. That's similar to the way God sees you. He thinks you are special—so much so that He sent His only Son to die for you in order to buy you back from the thief who tried to steal you from Him. (John 3:16.) He has made you His very own.

First Peter 2:9-10 says that you are "a chosen generation, a royal priesthood, an holy nation, a peculiar people...now the people of God...." You have been specifically chosen by God Himself to enter into a relationship with Him, and any sin in your life jeopardizes the strength of that relationship. That's why maintaining your virginity in all areas—spirit, soul, and body—is so important.

In order to maintain your virginity, you will need to know exactly what it is. Read on, and you may find that there is more to this treasure than you have realized in the past. Discover the telltale signs of virginity.

Chapter Two

Telltale Signs

Then the father of the young woman, and her mother, shall get and bring out the tokens of her virginity to the elders of the city at the gate. And her father shall say to the elders, I gave my daughter to this man as wife, but he hates and spurns her; and behold, he has made shameful charges against her, saying, I found not in your daughter the evidences of her virginity. And yet these are the tokens of my daughter's virginity. And they shall spread the garment before the elders of the city.

DEUTERONOMY 22:15-17 AMP

In the mid-80s Madonna's song "Like a Virgin" shot up the Billboard Top 10 list like a speeding bullet. In the song, she crooned about finding true love and how she felt every time a certain man touched her. While it was a catchy tune, it wasn't anywhere near the truth. The presence or absence of virginity is not measured by how you feel, but it is determined by how you think and what you do with those thoughts.

It's not easy to spot a virgin in today's society. They don't wear special clothes or elaborate hairstyles. There is no flashing neon sign over their heads announcing their decision to abstain from sex. Unfortunately, they don't walk around telling everyone the good news. Rather, people in our society seem to think that being a virgin is shameful.

It wasn't always that way. In fact, in the days of the Old Testament, virginity was highly prized and protected at all costs; and fornication (sex between two unmarried people) was an offense punishable by death! Not only did promiscuity bring shame upon the offender and his or her parent's household, but it was also an abomination to God. Simply put, fornication showed a serious lack of self-control and reverence for God.

If a woman was falsely accused of sexual impurity, her natural defense was a token, or proof, of her virginity.

You see, back in those days, when a man and a woman were married, a relative or appointed person waited outside the couple's bedroom to ensure the integrity of the bride's virginity. After the marriage was consummated, the groom would come out and hold up the sheet stained with his wife's blood. This proved that she had not lain with a man before the wedding. This fact was a source of pride and honor for her and her parents. It was especially meaningful for her father, for it proved that he had raised her up in the ways of the Lord and had done a good job of protecting her from other men. However, if the groom came out of the chamber and held up an unstained sheet, the family was shamed before the entire community and the woman stoned to death. (Deut. 22:20,21.)

If the husband waited a while before accusing his wife of being promiscuous (vv. 15-17), her fate depended on whether there was evidence, the stained bed sheet, to prove her virginity. If he were proven a liar, he not only paid a fine (100 shekels of silver) but also received a public whipping (vv. 18,19).

Today, no one stands outside of a newlywed's bedroom waiting for a bloodstained sheet. In fact, unless you are bold enough to ask someone if he or she is a virgin, chances are good that you won't be able to tell just by looking at the person. Some pretend to be virgins to get the "right" guy or girl, while others pretend not to be virgins to avoid the reputation of a "prude" or a "prig." In such a culture, how can we determine whether or not someone is a virgin?

The Real Deal

Technically, a virgin is someone who has never been physically intimate with another person. Obviously this excludes widows, widowers, divorcees, and prostitutes. However, a more accurate definition of a virgin would be someone who is physically, mentally, and spiritually pure. You may be thinking it's impossible to be that pure, but I assure you it isn't.

Most people believe that virginity has more to do with the physical realm than anything else, but that's not true. It involves one's total being. A person is not a virgin just because he or she hasn't had sex. Rather, a person is a virgin because he or she is pure in heart, mind, and body.

The heart, mind, and body are all intricately connected. When one part is affected, the others are too. It's similar to the way the parts of the body interact. For example, when you stub your toe, not only does your toe hurt but the pain shoots up your leg, registers in your brain, and comes out in a scream or groan. The apostle Paul, comparing the corporate church to the human body, said that "every joint supplieth" (Eph. 4:16); in other words, each part does its part and affects the whole. They all work together.

This same principle applies to virginity. The spirit, body, and soul (which is the mind, will, and emotions) affect a person's sexuality, and vice versa. It's impossible to maintain sexual intimacy without a unity of purpose among the spirit, soul, and body; and it's impossible to have sex with someone without the act also affecting your soul and spirit.

The Bible tells us that in the marriage relationship, a man and woman become one flesh, or one person. (Mark 10:7,8.) In other words, the sexual intimacy they share produces a unique closeness. No one else—with the exception of God—will ever know you as intimately as the person with whom you have sex. That's why God ordained sex to take place within the bounds of marriage. It is a holy thing to God and not something to be toyed with. Hebrews 13:4 AMP commands us to "...let the marriage bed be undefiled (kept undishonored); for God will judge and punish the unchaste [all guilty of sexual vice]...."

Fornication, which is sex between two unmarried people, grieves God because it causes both parties to be both physically and spiritually unclothed before Him. It rips off the protective covering of God's glory and presence from the two people and gives Satan greater access into their lives. (Eph. 4:27.)

That's why it is vitally important that you know how to protect all aspects of your virginity. It's not enough to abstain from sex. You must be able to recognize when it is under attack and know how to use God's natural and spiritual weapons of warfare to overcome the temptations of the enemy.

In the following chapter, you will see that God has given you specific tokens of virginity. These tokens will protect your virginity, and are therefore worth the effort to protect as well. Read on to discover the three powerful tokens of virginity.

Chapter Three

The Tokens of Virginity

I will establish My covenant or pledge with you.... And
God said, This is the token of the covenant (solemn pledge)
which I am making between Me and you and every living
creature that is with you, for all future generations: I set
My bow [rainbow] in the cloud, and it shall be a token or
sign of a covenant or solemn pledge between Me and the
earth. I will [earnestly] remember My covenant or solemn
pledge which is between Me and you and every living crea-
ture of all flesh....

GENESIS 9:11-13,15 AMP

A token is a distinguishing feature or characteristic. It
is also a symbol of protection and evidence of a relationship. The tokens, or symbols, of virginity distin-
guish the virgin from the non-virgin. They are evidence

of an intimate relationship with God and act as a protective barrier against sexual temptation.

To understand the concept of such tokens, consider a familiar tangible token within our culture—the wedding band. This ring tells those around the wearer that he or she is no longer "available" but has entered into a committed, long-term relationship with another person. The wedding band serves as a token, or a symbolic representation, of the covenant of marriage.

Likewise, the tokens of virginity are signs to God and humanity that you are a virgin, uncontaminated by the world and its views on sex.

A Sign to the World

If you do an in-depth study of the Bible, you'll discover that each promise God makes has a symbolic representation accompanying it. This symbol reminds both parties of the transaction that has taken place between them. For example, the rainbow symbolizes God's promise to Noah that He will never send floodwaters to destroy all flesh. (Gen. 9:11-13,15.) Abraham's circumcision was an outward sign of his separation unto God. (Gen. 17:10-14.) The lamb's blood on the doorframes of the Israelite homes served to remind them that they were God's chosen people, protected by the blood during Passover. (Ex. 12:13.)

A token, then, is evidence of a covenant relationship. This kind of relationship is sealed with blood and cannot be broken. If you are born again, you have a covenant relationship with God through the blood of Jesus. A covenant with God is a permanent, binding contract with no escape clauses. Of course, you may choose to walk away from the relationship, but God never will. His Word promises us that He is faithful and will never leave us or forsake us. (Heb. 13:5.)

A covenant token is not only evidence of the relationship between the two covenant partners but also, in covenants between God and people, a form of divine protection. For example, the token of being sealed with the Holy Spirit convinces us that we are children of God and protects us from an eternity in hell. (Eph. 1:13.) Likewise, the tokens of virginity are designed by God to protect us from worry, low self-esteem, rejection, disease, unexpected pregnancy, early death, and all the undesirable consequences of sexual sin.

Unfortunately, most people believe the lie that virginity is a barrier to fun, excitement, and pleasure. In truth, it is a gateway to peace, wholeness, and a sense of self worth. The tokens of virginity make the way toward the abundant life God has in mind for each of us.

The tokens of virginity that I've alluded to are purity, innocence, and the blood of Jesus. These elements work together to propel the virgin toward greater levels in God. The absence of any one of them allows the enemy to establish strongholds not easily destroyed except by the anointing (the burden-removing, bondage-destroying power) of God.

A better understanding of these tokens is vital to experiencing complete victory over sexual temptation. If you'll read on, you can start today to take the necessary steps to restoring, or simply protecting, your virginity— starting with the token of purity.

Chapter Four

Purity

For I am zealous for you with godly eagerness and a divine jealousy, for I have betrothed you to one Husband, to present you as a chaste virgin to Christ. But [now] I am fearful, lest that even as the serpent beguiled Eve by his cunning, so your minds may be corrupted and seduced from wholehearted and sincere and pure devotion to Christ.

2 Corinthians 11:2,3

The token, or protective seal, of purity is kept in the mind. If a person is not pure in thought, he or she will not be pure in deed. That is why the apostle Paul commanded us to think on things that are true, honest, just, pure, lovely, and of good report. (Phil. 4:8.) When our minds are fixed on the good things of God, the enemy has no choice but to leave.

Sin can't abide in God's presence, because His goodness eradicates sin. That's why God turned His back on Jesus when He was on the cross. (Matt. 27:45,46.) At that point Jesus *became sin*. If God had looked upon Jesus, being sin at that moment, Jesus would have been destroyed. Rather than destroy His Son, God turned away from Him.

When God faces sin, sin always loses. Therefore, when we practice the presence of God and maintain purity in heart, mind, and action, we have complete victory over sin. God's anointing—His power and presence—rests on us, giving us no-sweat victory over the temptation of the enemy.

Purity Is Essential

Purity is freedom from defilement or contamination. When something is contaminated it has been altered or changed—most often in a negative way.

When you are uncontaminated, your original created purpose—to serve God with your entire being—is kept intact. When we as Christians deposit the Word of God in our hearts, that Word purifies us. In other words, it rids us of contamination.

However, it's up to each of us to keep further contamination from entering. If we desire to maintain our virginity, we must not allow the world's view of sex to saturate our minds and defy what the Word of God has to say about it. When we allow a mistaken view of sex to get into our hearts, we corrupt the purity that God's Word has formed within us.

Over the years, I have counseled many young women who have lost their virginity prematurely. Most of these young ladies did not just see guys with the intention of giving up their virginity. The fact is that their virginity was long gone before they actually had sex with these young men. In other words, they acted out what was already in their minds.

Most Christians know that the Bible forbids sex outside of marriage, yet many Christians today seem to ignore the Scriptures pertaining to sex. Why do so few seem to overcome the temptation to sin sexually? Simply put, many lose the battle of keeping their minds focused on God and His Word.

Virginity as a Mindset

You see, virginity begins and ends in your mind, not your body. The same is true for any decision you make for God and against sin, or vice versa. Look, for example, at the first human battle against sin as seen in the lives of Adam and Eve.

In Genesis 2:16-17, we see God commanding Adam to refrain from eating the fruit of the tree in the middle of the Garden—the Tree of the Knowledge of Good and Evil. They were, however, free to eat the fruit of any of the other trees. The two had no trouble following this rule until Satan, speaking through a serpent, provoked them into disobeying God, as we see in Genesis 3:1-6:

> *Now the serpent was more subtil than any beast of the field which the Lord God had made. And he said unto the woman, Yea, hath God said, Ye shall not eat of every tree*

in the garden? And the woman said unto the serpent, We may eat of the fruit of the trees in the garden: But of the fruit of the tree which is in the midst of the garden, God hath said, Ye shall not eat of it, neither shall ye touch it, lest ye die. And the serpent said unto the woman, Ye shall not surely die: For God doth know that in the day ye eat thereof, then your eyes shall be opened, and ye shall be as gods, knowing good and evil. And when the woman saw that the tree was good for food, and that it was pleasant to the eyes, and a tree to be desired to make one wise, she took of the fruit thereof, and did eat, and gave also unto her husband with her; and he did eat.

The serpent challenged God's motives toward Adam and Eve, thereby planting doubt in their hearts. First, he questioned God's command, saying, "Yea, hath God said, Ye shall not eat of every tree of the garden?" (v. 1). Then he subtly accused God of trying to withhold information from them. "Ye shall not surely die: for God doth know that in the day ye eat thereof, then your eyes shall be opened, and ye shall be as gods, knowing good and evil" (Gen. 3:4,5). In essence he told them, "God lied to you. He knows you won't die. He's just trying to keep you from being like Him. He doesn't want you to have any power over your own life, so He's restricted you from eating of this tree."

The whole purpose of this speech was to push Adam and Eve out of the will of God. The serpent knew that if he could get them to question the validity of God's command, the natural end result would be their disobedience and sin. Ultimately, his theory proved to be true. Instead of rejecting the serpent's words and trusting in God, Adam and Eve entertained the thoughts he'd planted in their minds which directly contradicted God's words.

Genesis 3:6 says that when Eve "saw that the tree was good for food, and that it was pleasant to the eyes, and a tree desired to make one wise, she took of the fruit thereof...." In other words, Eve thought about the tree and what she could have if she ate its fruit. She did not just reach for the fruit without thinking about it. Instead, Eve paused to consider what the serpent had told her about the tree, and then she ate the fruit.

It's important to understand that the serpent did not just come right out and call God a liar. He just questioned God's intentions toward Adam and Eve.

Nevertheless, it was more than enough to cause them—two people who had walked with God and spent time in His presence daily—to sin.

Genesis 3:1 says, "Now the serpent was more subtil than any beast of the field which the Lord God had made." Subtle means "difficult to understand or perceive." It also means "to operate insidiously," or "to await a change to entrap."[1] In other words, unless there had been a neon sign over the serpent's head flashing the words "Danger! Don't believe this guy!" there was no way Adam and Eve could have seen what was coming.

Don't get me wrong: I'm not saying that striving for purity is easy. However, making a quality decision to practice purity and actively relying on the power of God will make the job easier. You see, Eve did not have to give in to the serpent's temptation. She could have cast down the doubts that arose in her mind and simply obeyed God, but she didn't. Instead, she entertained thoughts she shouldn't have and, as a result, sinned.

The same enemy who posed as the serpent in the Garden is roaming the earth today, seeking someone to destroy. (1 Peter 5:8.) Though he may not audibly speak, he uses a variety of methods to plant thoughts in people's minds that contradict God's Word.

He may be trying to speak to you through a billboard, commercial, boyfriend or girlfriend, or any of several (most likely unwitting) sources. The more you dwell on the thoughts that the enemy initiates through these sources, the greater will be the urge to act out on them. If you have found yourself thinking about things that oppose God's Word, the Bible, then your mind is going in the wrong direction—and the danger is that your body and spirit are likely to follow. If you've entertained lies about sex, then before you know it, you will end up participating in something that will leave you feeling used and rejected.

Maintain Your Focus

Many things in this world try to draw our focus and attention away from God: drugs, alcohol, entertainment, and relationships—just to name a few. Every step we take to or from these things begins and ends in the mind. Simply put, the mind is the battlefield on which Satan and God wage war for your life.

At times the battle must look like those television shows that portray a person with a devil sitting on one shoulder and an angel sitting on the other, each one trying to convince the person to do one thing or another.

Have you ever felt as though one voice in your brain was telling you to do one thing, and another was telling you to do the complete opposite? When that happens, even when we intend to do the right thing, it can sometimes be difficult to know for certain which voice to follow.

Eve made the mistake of turning away from the simplicity of God's command. You and I often do the same thing. For example, in 1 Corinthians 6:18, God commands us to flee, or run away from, sexual immorality because this is improper behavior for God's children. However, what usually happens is that we dutifully attend church and listen to a sermon on Sunday, then come home and allow the purity and simplicity of that message to become corrupted by what we hear, speak, and see. Then we wonder why we cave in under the pressure of temptation and fall into sin. The answer is obvious: In our minds, first, we simply did not hold on to the integrity of the Word of God.

Here is an example of how this can affect you in your dating relationships. Your boyfriend may tell you, "You know, Baby, you look really good when you swing your hips," or "I really like the way you look in that dress." You like the attention you're receiving, so you start dressing and walking to please him. Before you know it, you're consistently disobeying God's command to "abstain from all appearance of evil" (1 Thess. 5:22), carrying yourself in a way that displeases Him. Your purity has already been corrupted. You now prefer pleasing a person to pleasing God, though sex has not even entered the picture.

Several outside influences will rob you of your purity if you are not careful to recognize and avoid them. Three of the most common pitfalls are the wrong kinds of music, television shows, and conversations.

I was at the gym the other day and heard a song on the radio that said, "He's just my baby's daddy." In other words, "He's in my bed, but he doesn't really mean anything to me. He's just the father of my baby." Over the years I've come to the realization that the large majority of secular songs are about one of two things: someone cheating on someone else, or two people in a sexual relationship. Sure, they have a nice rhythm and beat; but their value must be weighed against the value of a pure mind, heart, and body.

It's pretty difficult to stay pure by attacking Satan with the Word of God if we haven't been depositing it in our hearts. We cannot listen to secular music and expect to be able to resist Satan when he comes to attack our purity. Instead of remembering Scriptures, we'll only remember all the secular lyrical philosophies we've been listening to.

Equally disarming is watching television shows that impose worldly views on sex. I'm convinced there are shows on television that come straight from the pit of hell. I've seen episodes where the actors were competing to get rid of their virginity. You can't watch stuff like that and think your virginity is going to stay intact, because little by little your thinking will change. Instead of meditating on the fact that God said your body is the temple of the Holy Spirit (1 Cor. 6:19), you'll be thinking, *I wonder how long it will take me to get rid of my virginity.*

Another way to jeopardize your purity is to engage in illicit conversations about sex.

How many times have you or your friends made a comment about the opposite sex? "Oh, man, she's so fine!" or "Girl, look at his butt. He's looking good in those jeans!"

Do you frequently talk about sex or physical attractions? Jesus made it clear in Matthew 12:34 that what comes out of your mouth is what is in your heart. Your words reflect what you think about, and what you think about affects who you become.

King David, a man after God's own heart, had his purity corrupted by lustful thoughts. Second Samuel 11:2-5 says that he committed adultery with a woman he had observed bathing at night. Notice that I used the word *observed*. He didn't just take a quick glance and then repent. Instead, David watched intently and then chose to dwell on what he'd seen.

That's where many of us go wrong. We dwell on the negative and ungodly things we see and hear daily. This only leads to sin. It causes us to doubt the truth of God's Word and question His motives toward us. In other words, it causes us to begin to believe Satan's lie that God is trying to spoil our fun. Eventually, if we continue to focus on the lie, we put action to our thoughts in pursuit of the proposed pleasure. Sadly, though, once we've acted on the lie, the lingering feeling is not pleasure but guilt.

By concentrating more on what God desires for us *to* have instead of on what we should *not* have, we'll begin to walk more confidently, knowing that we can successfully resist any weapon or temptation of the enemy. That's when we'll be able to pray from our hearts, just as David did, "Let the words of my mouth, and the meditation of my heart, be acceptable in thy sight, O Lord, my strength, and my redeemer" (Ps. 19:14).

Do you desire to please the Lord with your life by protecting your virginity? Then commit today with the simple step of protecting the first token of virginity— your purity. Regardless of what your sexual past may look like, it is never too late to take this first step by saturating your heart and soul with God's Word. Neither is it ever too late to discover and protect the second token of virginity—your innocence.

Chapter Five

Innocence

*"...but I want you to be wise about what is good, and
innocent about what is evil."*

ROMANS 16:19 NIV

Our judicial system is based on the idea that a person
is innocent until proven guilty. However, the word *innocent* is very rarely used when describing the people
around us. To be innocent means to be free from guilt or
sin, especially through lack of knowledge of evil. An
innocent person has a clear conscience because he or she
has committed no wrongdoing.

The concept of innocence is especially important in a
court of law. The primary responsibility of a prosecuting
attorney is to prove, beyond a shadow of a doubt, that

the man or woman claiming to be innocent really is not, but rather that the accused knew he or she was breaking the law. On the other hand, the defense attorney must prove his or her client's innocence—that the accused had no knowledge whatsoever of the crime and is innocent of the charges. If the defense attorney is unsuccessful in pleading the client's case, the accused will be punished.

A Powerful Agent

Innocence, like a good defense attorney, is a powerful agent that works together with purity to protect you from the devil's lie that you cannot remain a virgin. Innocence protects your virginity against sexual temptation and sin. It resides in your mind, just as purity does, and is triggered by thoughts and experiences. When you are innocent, your mind is free from the guilt that often accompanies evil thoughts, desires, and actions. In other words, you lack the knowledge and experience that come with living by the world's standards.

Innocence is best seen in young children. Because they haven't lived long enough to gain much experience, they have an unrealistic concept of many things—including money, time, and even the consequences of their actions.

As a child, were you ever concerned about what might happen if you ate a piece of unwrapped candy that you found on the sidewalk? Did you consider the risks of crossing the street without looking or opening the front door to a stranger? Most likely, you did not.

Being innocent means that you have absolutely no knowledge of evil. Let me explain how this works in a sexual sense. When you leave one relationship as a virgin and get involved in another, the devil cannot accuse you of sinning, because you are innocent. In other words, you are guilty of no wrongdoing. On the other hand, if you had sex in the first relationship, Satan could now enter into this new relationship and accuse you of wrongdoing. In fact, he can bring enough guilt for you to believe that it is only right for you to have sex in this new relationship.

Think back to the last time your parents accused you of doing something you did not do. What happened?

Chances are good that you tried to defend yourself. If you were innocent, you had the confidence to stand up for yourself; however, if you were guilty, the confidence to prove your innocence was not there within you, making it difficult to press on.

A Shield Against Corruption

Similarly, innocence plays a vital role in helping you press on and maintain your virginity. If you are guilty of leading someone on or allowing him or her to touch your intimate parts, it will be difficult to say no when the other person wants to go further. However, by remaining innocent, you will be able to boldly resist the temptation to sin sexually.

What most people fail to realize is that the things they hear, see, and say can easily destroy their innocence. These influences, if they project anything but the truth, can corrode the conscience. It may be subtle, but the corrosion process, left unchecked, will eventually affect a person's whole being.

For example, let's say you choose to listen to your friends' sex stories instead of meditating on God's Word. You begin frequently thinking about the subject of sex. Before you know it, your knowledge of sex has increased to the point that, even if you are still technically a virgin, the things you say and do fool everyone into believing you're not. Your innocence is destroyed little by little as your mind dwells more on the evil that you can do than on the good, and eventually your body follows your mind into sin.

Innocence is the key to a clear conscience. It frees you from the usual fear, worry, and doubt that come with sin. When you are free from the guilt of sin, your conscience is clear. There is nothing in your heart to make you feel fearful or worried about the natural consequences of sin. There is nothing to make you feel doubtful of your innocence.

True virgins are innocent. That doesn't mean they are perfect; neither does it mean they are ignorant. It just means they do not allow their thoughts or their consciences to be corrupted by worldly thinking.

Not having a working knowledge of evil isn't the same as not knowing what evil is.

In Matthew 10:16, Jesus commanded us to be as wise as serpents, but innocent as doves. That means we are to know what evil is, but stay away from it.

Look at how people approach alcohol, for example. Everyone has been warned about the dangers of drinking, but just because we know about the dangers doesn't always mean we stay away from them. Think about how many alcohol-related deaths occur annually due to drunk driving or toxic levels of alcohol in the bloodstream. Nevertheless, most people ignore the warnings and do as they please.

This is what Jesus was warning us about. Christians are not supposed to find out about something evil and participate in it to see if it really is bad for them. That's foolishness. Wisdom says, "I see that is dangerous. I'd better stay away from it; otherwise, it'll hurt me."

Innocence protects the soul—the place where your mind, will, and emotions reside. It keeps you from having to reap the negative, and often painful, consequences associated with wrong choices and actions.

Such consequences include the emotions of guilt, shame, and sadness.

Innocence not only protects you from negative emotions, but it also strengthens your character. Your lifestyle reflects who you are. If you walk in the presence of God daily by thinking about God and His Word, praying, reading your Bible and practicing what it teaches, your life will reflect that time spent with Him. Just as Moses' face reflected the glory of God (Ex. 34:29), your life and personality will also do the same.

Innocence gives glory and credibility to God and His servants. Have you ever found yourself needing to repair the damage other Christians have caused because of their weak witness and ungodly lifestyles? When Christians misrepresent their Lord, it makes sharing Christ with the lost all the more difficult. However, when God's children walk with Him, obeying His Word, their lives draw people to Him.

In light of this fact, it is important to remember that righteous thinking leads to righteous actions. In other words, if you will keep your mind on the goodness of God, your life will reflect that goodness. It is also important to realize that your innocence is the key to both righteous thinking and righteous actions.

Innocence protects the mind and body from temptation and self-deception. It prevents you from keeping your mind on improper thoughts. It keeps you from participating in activities that will eventually cause you to sin.

You must understand that Satan will attack your mind before he'll attack your body. He does this because he knows if he can gain control of your mind, then your body will follow. You will never be able to know or fulfill God's plan for your life if your mind is messed up with ungodly thoughts. (Rom. 12:1,2.)

Think about the windshield of a car. You can't drive safely if you can't see the road ahead of you, and you can't see the road ahead if your windows are covered with mud. What you need to do is wash your windows so you can see to drive.

The same principle applies to your life. You can't stay away from sin if you can't see the way that God wants you to go, and you can't see that path if your mental vision is smeared by sinful thoughts. When you cleanse your mind daily with the Word of God, you are able to see the path that God has paved for you and keep sinful thoughts from obstructing your vision.

The Road to Holiness

When innocence is at work in your life, your thoughts and actions are aligned with the Word of God, because it is the final authority in your life. Nothing and no one can take its place. This is what leads to *holiness,* which is hating what God hates and loving what He loves.

Job 17:8 AMP says, "...the innocent shall stir himself up against the godless and polluted." When your character and thinking reflect what is written in the Word, sinful things bother you. Provocative clothes, suggestive music, and sexual innuendoes make you feel uncomfortable. You are no longer able to live according to the world's standards because you are no longer in agreement with the world. You are no longer equipped to live as the world lives. To try to continue to live as though you were of the world—ignoring the voice of the Holy Spirit and deliberately placing yourself in the way of temptation and sin—would be hypocrisy.

Hypocrisy is one way to stop the blessings of God from manifesting in your life. Hypocrisy is pretending to be someone or something you are not. Simply put, hypocrisy is lying.

If you call yourself a Christian and yet choose to live by worldly standards, you are a liar. Ephesians 5:8 tells us that once we become born again, we no longer belong to this world, but to God. We have been brought out of darkness and into the light. To pretend we are not God's children when we are is like a slap in the face to Him. (Heb. 6:4-6.)

The world is anything but innocent. It is a system run by Satan himself, "the god of this world" (2 Cor. 4:4). To participate in the activities he's established is to wind up outside of the perfect will of God for your life.

Innocence prevents you from participating in activities that God does not sanction. It's hard for a holy God to bless someone covered in sin. That's why, as was mentioned in a previous chapter, God turned away from Jesus when He was dying on the cross. Second

Corinthians 5:21 says Jesus was made sin for us. In other words, He became the personification of evil. Although the end result was eternal life for us, God still had to turn away from His own Son. If he hadn't, His anointing (the burden-removing, bondage-destroying power) would have destroyed the sin, and Jesus along with it.

Innocence destroys the power of sin and enables you to lift up your head without shame or fear, because deep down you know that your conscience is clear and you are free from sin. Psalm 32:2 NIV says, "Blessed is the man whose sin the Lord does not count against him and in whose spirit is no deceit." God empowers those who live holy lives before Him. When we make a quality decision to protect our innocence, we make a way for the blessings of God to overrun our lives.

Maintaining your innocence is similar to keeping a white shirt clean while working in a pigsty: It's difficult but not impossible. It all depends on how you approach the task. If you work hard, chances are good that your beautiful shirt will be black with grime in a matter of minutes. On the other hand, if you work smart, your shirt will remain spotless.

The key to "working smart" and maintaining your innocence is found in the Word of God. It is only by diligently and consistently studying the Word that you find the heavenly barriers you need to defend your innocence and keep your mind, spirit, and body clean. Read on and you will discover the third barrier and token—the blood.

Chapter Six

The Blood

"As for the life of all flesh, the blood of it represents the life of it...."

LEVITICUS 17:14 AMP

Blood has always symbolized life. Everything you need to survive flows through the millions of blood vessels in your body. Red blood cells deliver oxygen, water, and nutrients to your internal organs and carry waste material to the lungs and kidneys. At the same time, millions of white blood cells fight off the harmful germs and bacteria we daily come into contact with, including potential diseases that might otherwise kill us. We can even give our blood away in order to save another person's life. That's why the Red Cross sponsors so many blood drives each year, and it's also why doctors have a patient's blood type on standby during an operation: A loss of blood signifies a loss of life.

God has designed us to be completely dependent upon blood. Some people may think that oxygen and water are the most important things in the world, but that is not true. You could drink all the water in the world, but without blood cells to break it down and carry it around the body, you would be wasting your time.

Babies in the womb depend entirely upon their mother's blood for survival. Everything she takes into her body is passed through the umbilical cord—the only connection her child has to oxygen and nutrients.

A Dual Purpose

In addition to providing vital nutrients to our organs, blood also protects us from sexually transmitted infection and disease. The hymen, a thin membrane that partly covers the opening to a woman's vagina, protects the uterus from anything that could cause an infection or bring disease to that area of the body. When a virgin has sexual intercourse for the first time, blood is shed, signifying the tearing of the hymen. Now, physically speaking, the woman is no longer considered a virgin, and her body becomes vulnerable to diseases it never was before—diseases such as syphilis, gonorrhea, and herpes. In addition, her risk for urinary tract and yeast infections increases, as does the chance of pregnancy.

Physically, then, blood offers women protection against disease. However, spiritually and mentally, it offers something more—protection against shame, rejection, and the consequences of sin in the heart and mind. The shedding of blood through sexual intercourse signifies the end of virginity; or, in the case of fornication, the end of the protective covering of God's presence and power. Just as with any other sin, fornication leaves a person spiritually naked.

In a spiritually naked state, a person cannot please God. This is why God sent Jesus to earth—to clothe us permanently with God's glory. God originally created humanity to wear His glory always. However, Adam and

Eve's disobedience removed the glory of God from their lives, revealing their physical nakedness for the first time.

> *And the eyes of them both were opened, and they knew that they were naked; and they sewed fig leaves together, and made themselves aprons. And they heard the voice of the Lord God walking in the garden in the cool of the day: and Adam and his wife hid themselves from the presence of the Lord God amongst the trees of the garden. And the Lord God called unto Adam and said unto him, Where art thou? And he said, I heard thy voice in the garden, and I was afraid, because I was naked; and I hid myself. And he said, Who told thee that thou wast naked? Hast thou eaten of the tree, whereof I commanded thee that thou shouldst not eat?*
>
> GENESIS 3:7-13

Because of their sin, Adam and Eve were filled with shame and fear—two things that cannot abide in the presence of God. Prior to this incident, Adam and Eve were both naked and unashamed. (Gen. 2:25.) However, after their disobedience, the Bible says that their eyes were opened (Gen. 3:7) and they realized what they had done. Adam and Eve had jumped to a level of existence they were not ready for. Ironically, neither one would confess the sin, and neither one was mature enough to handle the consequences. Instead, each one of them tried to pin the blame on someone or something else. In the end, God had no choice but to punish them for their disobedience by sending them—in their spiritual nakedness—out of the Garden.

Human beings were never designed to live outside of God's protective covering, yet many Christians today walk around spiritually naked. For some, the reason lies in their inability to commit to Christ wholeheartedly. For others, it is the result of habitual sin, or iniquity.

Yet spiritual nakedness is the very thing that brought Jesus to earth to begin with. By dying on the cross, He took our place and put us in His position, thus providing us with the clothing of God's glory once again. Now, in Revelation 3:18 Jesus warns His body, the church, not to be found spiritually naked, saying, "...buy...white raiment, that thou mayest be clothed, and that the shame of thy nakedness do not appear...."

We remain clothed in "white raiment" by avoiding sin—including sexual sin.

An Abomination to God

The reason fornication is such an abomination to God is that it tramples on something He considers holy—the marriage bed. Paul warns us in Hebrews 13:4 to keep the marriage bed pure and undefiled. To defile means to make impure or unclean by contact.

When people have sex outside of marriage, they mock a holy act—an act that has been set apart for a special purpose. Sexual intercourse joins a husband and wife together in a way that can never be duplicated. In God's eyes, the two become one person. To carelessly disregard that ideal is to insult the One who instituted the practice to begin with.

Fornication is the final stage in the loss of virginity. For a woman, the physical barrier designed to protect her against disease is broken down. However, a mental and spiritual breakdown happens before a physical change. Fornication means that a couple has allowed Satan to break down the purity and innocence God put in place to defend them from sin. As a result, they open themselves up to a new "hunger"—the hunger for physical gratification—that the enemy works tirelessly to feed.

The result of fornication is the same today as it was in the Old Testament. It removes the glory of God from our lives and covers us with sin and the residue of the world. It opens us up to ideas and ways that are opposed to God and His Word, and it defiles our physical bodies. Instead of our lives overflowing with the blessings and abundance of God, we end up having to bear the consequences that come from our poor choices: sickness, depression, insecurity, disappointment, and even bitterness.

God never intended for anyone to experience sex outside of the protective bounds of marriage. He never intended for us to have to deal with the consequences associated with fornication. He did not design us to live a life separated from Him by our own sin.

However, because of our constant disobedience to His commands, He has no choice but to let us experience the consequences of our actions. Numbers 23:19 says, "God is not a man, that he should lie; neither the son of man, that he should repent: hath he said, and shall he not do it? or hath he spoken, and shall he not make it good?"

Therefore, God being faithful to His Word, must allow us to experience the consequences of our sin.

The good news is that it's never too late to begin again with God. He wants His children to walk with Him daily and experience the abundant life He promised us. The only thing required of us is that we align with His Word and commit to follow Him wholeheartedly.

In the following chapter, you will see how you can start aligning with God's Word and following Him by defending the castle of your virginity.

Chapter Seven

Defending Your Castle

*"Do not be conformed to this world (this age), [fash-
ioned after and adapted to its external, superficial
customs], but be transformed (changed) by the [entire]
renewal of your mind [by its new ideals and its new atti-
tude], so that you may prove [for yourselves] what is the
good and acceptable and perfect will of God...."*

ROMANS 12:2 AMP

In the Middle Ages, when a king desired a particular
piece of land, he would mount a siege against the castle
that presided over it. Siege warfare required persistence.
Castles were well fortified and could stand direct attack
for long periods of time. Some were equipped with
secret passages, underground tunnels, and even "murder

holes"—openings in walls and floors used to hide sharp-shooters prepared to kill attackers unfortunate enough to get inside.

Yet despite its massiveness and the defense of an enormous army, a castle could very rarely survive a siege. In a siege, the attackers surrounded the building, effectively preventing any supplies or reinforcements from reaching the castle. It took weeks, even months, to gain control of the property. By the time the siege was over, the inhabitants of the castle were either weak or dead from starvation, disease, or severe wounds.

Satan works in much the same way in his attack against a person's virginity. His method of attack is to surround and conquer. Persistence is the key element in his activity. He does not attack once and then sit back and wait for something to happen. Just as a wrecking ball cannot tear down a building by hitting a wall just once but strikes until the wall breaks apart and falls down, the devil tries to strike until all of our defenses break down.

It's so important to make sure that we do not allow him an opportunity to establish a stronghold in our lives. Once it's there, it's difficult, though not impossible, to get out.

It's important to remember that temptation is almost always subtle. There won't be a flashing neon sign over it that says "Temptation here!" The Bible tells us that Satan masquerades as an angel of light. (2 Cor. 11:14.) That means that anything he uses, even those things that appear to be good, can be used for evil. Satan uses these subtle means of warfare because he is in no real hurry to see us fall into sin. In his siege warfare, persistence is his key weapon.

We Must Renew Our Minds

Renewing our minds is essential if we want to protect our castle—our purity, innocence, and blood—from caving in to demonic attack. To renew simply means to make new again. When we renew our minds, we retrain ourselves to think about things that pertain to God.

If we want to renew our physical appearance by losing some weight, for instance, we have to train our bodies to exercise regularly and eat food that is nutritious. It's not easy—sometimes we might slip up and binge on a brownie or conveniently forget to go to the gym—but in the end, our diligence pays off. Our bodies slim down, our endurance levels soar, and our mouths and stomachs get used to eating certain foods.

The same is true of our minds. The more our minds focus on Jesus, the stronger they become against diversions from the renewal process. Thus, it becomes much more difficult for the enemy to come in and plant wicked thoughts there.

The mind is like an expensive house. Such a house attracts all kinds of people, especially thieves. However, a thief cannot break into a house unless a way has been made for him. If the homeowner neglects to turn on the alarm, the thief can come in and steal whatever he finds there. However, if the gates are locked and the alarm is on, the burglar doesn't stand a chance.

In the house of your mind, you must be careful to keep the spiritual alarm of the voice of the Holy Spirit set. The moment you let your mind settle on ungodly thoughts, you turn off your spiritual alarm and allow Satan to come in and rob you of your purity. Then once your purity is gone, it's very difficult to get back without a fight.

You may say, "If that's the case, I just won't allow these thoughts to come into my mind!" That's a great idea—and when you figure out how to do that, please let me know. However, whether we like it or not, wicked thoughts are bound to come. It's what we do with those thoughts that matters.

Paul tells us in 2 Corinthians 10:5 how we are to handle these thoughts, saying, "[Cast] down imaginations, and every high thing that exalteth itself against the knowledge of God, and [bring] into captivity every thought to the obedience of Christ...." In other words, we must do everything within our power to avoid dwelling on things that may cause us to fall away from God's will for our lives.

Five Ways To Preserve Virginity

Here are five ways to defend the fortress of our minds, and therefore, to preserve our virginity.

Meditate Daily on God's Word

The best way to protect your mind is to meditate on God's Word. To meditate means to ponder or dwell upon. Psalm 119:9 NIV says, "How can a young man keep his way pure? By living according to your word." Proverbs 30:5 NIV tells us that "every word of God is flawless; he is a shield to those who take refuge in him." Only the purity and truth of the Word can protect you against the onslaught of the enemy.

The strength of that Word is what Jesus used when He was tempted, as recorded in Matthew 4:1-11. Every time the devil tried to tempt Jesus with thoughts of power, position, and wealth, Jesus responded with the Word of God.

The Word is the ultimate source of authority and power, for it is God, as John 1:1 says: "In the beginning was the Word, and the Word was with God, and the Word was God." Therefore, every time Jesus quoted Scripture, He reminded the devil that he had no real power or authority to back up what he was offering. Not only that, but there was no room in Jesus' mind for

Satan's thoughts, because it overflowed with the truth of God's Word.

Likewise, no temptation or trap the enemy sends our way can harm us when we meditate on the Word of God. The doubt, fear, and disbelief the devil tries to plant in our minds disintegrate because that space is already taken up.

It's important to remember that every thought we dwell on ultimately results in action, whether positive or negative. By meditating on the truth of Scripture, we develop the character and mind of Christ. You may wonder if that's possible. Philippians 2:5 says, "Let this mind be in you, which was also in Christ Jesus...." If it weren't possible, we wouldn't have been commanded to seek after it. Anything is possible with God. Once you purpose to align your thinking with His Word, you will be able to overcome the enemy instead of the enemy overcoming you.

Consistently Spend Time in God's Word

Consistently spending time in God's Word is the second way to guard our minds and virginity. Consistency is the key to breakthrough. Every time we choose not to spend consistent quality time with God, we give the enemy an entrance into our lives. Jesus illustrated this principle in the Gospel of Luke.

> "When an evil spirit comes out of a man, it goes through arid places seeking rest and does not find it. Then it says, 'I will return to the house I left.' When it arrives, it finds the house swept clean and put in order. Then it goes and takes seven other spirits more wicked than itself, and they go in and live there. And the final condition of that man is worse than the first."
>
> LUKE 11:24-26 NIV

When we study the Word every other day, every other week, or only during a crisis, we leave the door wide open for Satan to come in and plant ungodly thoughts in our minds. In other words, we do exactly what the man did in Jesus' illustration—clean the house, but leave it empty. We must fill our minds with Scripture. Otherwise, the only thing we will be doing is falling right back into the same bondage we're trying to get out of.

Obey the Word

The third way we can protect our minds and virginity is to obey God by doing what the Word tells us to do. If it commands us to abstain from fornication, then we must do it. We cannot experiment here and there. To do so would be like sticking our toes in a tank full of hungry sharks just to see if they'll get bitten off: It would be foolishness.

Obedience to God is the only way to show we love Him. Believe it or not, He's not impressed with how long we can pray in the Spirit or how many people have been healed when we prayed for them. Jesus said in John 14:15 that we show Him love by keeping His commandments. Likewise, James 1:22 NIV commands us not to "merely listen to the word" but to "do what it says."

We are sadly mistaken if we think we can go to church, call ourselves Christians, and then sleep around with whomever we want to. The Scripture continues by saying that when we do this we are "like a man who looks at his face in a mirror, and, after looking at himself, goes away and immediately forgets what he looks like. But the man who looks intently into the perfect law...not forgetting what he has heard, but doing it—he will be blessed in what he does" (vv. 23-25).

To be blessed means to be empowered to prosper and excel. The more we obey God, the more He showers His blessings on us. When we do what His Word tells us to do, we succeed in everything we put our hands to.

Joseph demonstrated what this Scripture means. Whether he was in the field reaping the harvest, in jail, or serving in Pharaoh's court, he succeeded in everything he did. (Gen. 37-41.) He was blessed because he obeyed God.

Resist Peer Pressure

The fourth key to protecting our minds and virginity is to resist peer pressure. When I was a child, my mother would always ask me a question that reminded me not to buckle under peer pressure. She would say, "Carla, if your friends jump off a bridge, are you going to jump, too?"

It's foolish to participate in ungodly activities just because everyone else is doing so. We must be careful whom we listen to and hang out with. First Corinthians 15:33 AMP says, "Evil companionships (communion, associations) corrupt and deprave good manners and morals and character." This means we have to make a choice. If we are hanging out with people who are having illicit sex, telling dirty jokes, and sharing sex stories, we must choose between protecting our purity and their companionship.

That's not to say we should never speak to them again or begin treating them as if they had a contagious disease. It just means that there is a line that neither we nor they can cross, because the longer we continue to associate with them, the greater our chances become of caving in to temptation and sin.

One rumor that has been around as long as I can remember has been a trap for many well-meaning virgins. That rumor is that "everyone is doing it." Ironically, it's not true. Thousands of teens and young adults today are virgins. Though you'd never know it by the way people talk about it, virginity is not a rare thing.

While it helps to know you're not alone, the best cure for peer pressure is the confidence that comes from knowing that God has a plan for your life. (Jer. 29:11.)

That plan can only come through an intimate knowledge of Him and His Word.

Practice God's Presence

The fifth way to protect our minds and virginity is to practice the presence of God. Jesus said in Matthew 24:36 that no man knows the day or the hour of His return, except the Father. That means we must be ready for His return at all times.

In addition, Paul commands us, "...since we are surrounded by so great a cloud of witnesses...let us strip off and throw aside every encumbrance (unnecessary weight) and the sin which so readily (deftly and cleverly) clings to and entangles us..." (Heb. 12:1 AMP). In other words, everyone in heaven can see the things we say and do.

Whatever we do in secret or in the dark can always be seen by this heavenly audience. Practicing the presence of God simply means becoming aware of that audience, specifically of God Himself. Pulling the wool over our mothers' eyes is easy, but it's God we have to be concerned about. He gives us everything we need for successful

Christian living, and all He asks in return is for us to show Him love by obeying His commandments.

It's important that we practice the presence of God daily, because it will keep us out of trouble and in the center of God's perfect will for our lives. If we will do so, we will become so concerned with Him that we'll forget all about doing things that go against His Word. First John 3:3 says that those who keep their minds on Jesus stay in a constant state of purity. They avoid falling prey to the devil by staying in the Word of God and obeying what it says. It's that simple.

A Strong Defense

The tokens of purity, innocence, and the blood work together to form a strong line of defense against attacks on virginity. When one of them is damaged or missing, we open the door for Satan to come in and destroy us by whatever means he has at his disposal. We must remember our physical purity (the blood) is protected by our mental purity. In other words, once we've obtained mental experience in sexual matters, it's not long before we begin to get that same experience physically.

Therefore, consistently remaining in the Word of God is the key to successfully defending our castle. It contains everything we need to overcome every demonic attack. However, it won't work if we don't spend quality time getting those Scriptures into our hearts and minds, where the battle takes places.

You don't have to be a casualty of war. Make a quality decision today to put these steps into practice, and confidently say, "The Lord God will help me; therefore shall I not be confounded: therefore have I set my face like a flint, and I know that I shall not be ashamed" (Isa. 50:7). It's never too late to start!

Chapter Eight

A New Beginning

"Remember ye not the former things, neither consider the things of old. Behold, I will do a new thing; now it shall spring forth; shall ye not know it? I will even make a way in the wilderness, and rivers in the desert."

ISAIAH 43:18,19

You may be thinking, *I've already lost my virginity! What do I do now?* The good news is that it's never too late to make a quality decision to walk by the Word of God. Although your physical purity may be gone, you can be made new mentally, emotionally, and spiritually. However, the only way to be made new is not by following a checklist or by waving a magic wand. The key is found in the blood of Jesus.

Here is a true slogan: "Christians aren't perfect; they're just forgiven." No one is perfect except Jesus, the Son of God. That is why we need Him so desperately.

Sadly, most of us became Christians after the damage to our minds and bodies was already done and there was nothing left to try except Jesus. I've seen it over and over again in my counseling sessions with young women. By the time they come in to see me, they are discouraged, defeated, and without hope. My office represents their last-ditch effort to save self-esteem and, at times, even their relationship with God.

A Never-Ending Cycle

These women, like many other people, feel trapped in a never-ending cycle of sin. They try to overcome a spiritual problem through fleshly means. However, it's impossible to protect the tokens of virginity without the support that comes from the Word of God. The battle is one that takes place in the mind, not on a literal battlefield. Therefore, whenever you try to accomplish something in your own strength, it fails. The only thing that endures is what is done through Christ. His strength is never-failing; ours is fragile and short-lived.

The apostle Paul understood this. In fact, he faced the same problem in his own life. Even after he evangelized most, if not all, of the Mediterranean, he still struggled with the desires of his flesh. He said, "I find then a law, that, when I would do good, evil is present with me...warring against the law of my mind, and bringing me into captivity to the law of sin which is in my members. O wretched man that I am! who shall deliver me from the body of this death? I thank God through Jesus Christ our Lord" (Rom. 7:21,23-25).

Jesus Is the Way

It is only through and by the blood of Jesus that we are strengthened, justified, and made whole. (Rom. 5:9.) This is because He took our sin and its consequences upon Himself in order to give us the opportunity to receive eternal life. In other words, by shedding His blood, Jesus brought salvation to humankind. Salvation, or *soteria* in the original Greek, means "soundness of mind, safety, deliverance and health."[1] The blood of Jesus does not just cover our sin; it completely destroys it and makes us whole (sound, safe, delivered, and healthy).

We no longer have to struggle with the guilt and shame of the past. It's ridiculous to carry that weight around when God no longer has a record of it. When we accept Jesus Christ as our Lord and Savior, we are also accepting the rights and privileges that come with being children of God: forgiveness of sin, intimacy with the Father, health, wholeness, angelic protection, and supernatural provision. The blood of Jesus contains everything we need to help us live holy and pleasing lives before God.

The path to restoring our virginity is not a difficult one to take. It simply involves a quality decision to turn away from sin and toward an intimate relationship with Christ. This does not mean that He erases any memories we may have of sin. It simply means we allow Him to restore our purity through His Word and to wipe away our sins in order to make us innocent and blameless before God. It also means He covers us with His blood, replacing the physical blood shed while we were in sin. As a result, our spiritual and physical nakedness is covered.

Mark 10:27 tells us that nothing is impossible for God. His power and ability know no bounds. It's our own insecurity and doubt that try to prevent us from taking full advantage of the cleansing power of His blood. Decide today to live a life of discipline by walking in the truth of God's Word. When you do this, you'll discover that the abundance of His blessings outweighs the challenges of daily living.

If you want to start over again, experiencing the power of God's grace to renew your virginity, I welcome you to say this prayer now:

Heavenly Father, I thank You for the understanding You have given me regarding my virginity. I repent right now for entertaining thoughts that go against Your Word, and for acting out on those thoughts. I know now that my purity and innocence, together with the blood of Jesus, protect me from temptation and sin. Thank You for showing me how to live a life that is holy, honorable, and pleasing in Your sight. I make a decision to align my thoughts and actions with Your Word, and I submit my will to Yours. I receive Your forgiveness now, and thank You in advance for a clean heart and a new beginning. I declare this to be so now, in Jesus' name. Amen.

If you prayed that prayer, you can start today to live the life of a virgin, cherishing the tokens of this most precious gift—purity, innocence, and the blood of Jesus that makes you whole again.

Conclusion

Put on God's whole armor [the armor of a heavy-armed soldier which God supplies], that you may be able success-fully to stand up against [all] the strategies and the deceits of the devil.

EPHESIANS 6:11 AMP

Virginity is not lost overnight. It takes time for its protective barriers to break down or disappear altogether.

When a farmer plants seed in the ground, he doesn't stand over them with a watering can shouting, "Grow!" Instead, he fertilizes the soil and waters it, watching carefully to make sure the seeds have everything they need to grow into healthy plants. Eventually the ground breaks, and the first little bit of green pops out. After a while, the seeds mature and bear fruit.

Every farmer is aware of the dangers his seeds face. Insects, disease, inclement weather, and toxic chemicals are just a few of the obstacles that must be overcome in order for the seeds to produce a large harvest. Seeds are extremely temperamental. Any sudden change in their environment can prove deadly. That's why farmers give their seed a great deal of attention. They must protect them at all costs if they want to see results.

In the spirit, Satan plants seeds—thoughts—in your mind and heart. He fertilizes them through the things you hear and see daily, whether through television shows, movies, music, stories, or jokes that degrade sex and portray it as just another leisure activity. Before you know it, the seeds can bear fruit that will rob you of your virginity and hurt your relationship with God.

Satan expects a return—the loss of your virginity—based on the seeds he sows into your life. Every day he subtly chips away at your resistance until the tokens protecting you from temptation have been removed, causing you to sin.

Maintain Your Tokens

The Word of God and the blood of Jesus are the most powerful weapons you have against demonic attack, but they only work when you align yourself with the Scriptures and apply the blood of Jesus over your life. Don't wait until the last second—when you find yourself balanced precariously on the edge of sin—to run to God. Discipline and consistency are the keys to maintaining the tokens of your virginity. The earlier you begin to guard your heart and mind, the better off you'll be.

Decide today to use the heavenly weapons at your disposal. Take an offensive, rather than a defensive, stance against the attack of the enemy. The Word of God promises that if you resist the devil, he will flee from you. (James 4:7.) Resist the thief with the Word and with the three tokens that God has given you to maintain your virginity—purity, innocence, and the blood. With them, you will overcome every temptation to sin and experience the abundant life that God has prepared for you.

Study Questions

Chapter 1

What's the Big Deal Anyway?

1. What is your idea of the "ideal woman"? In what ways (physical, mental, social, or emotional) are you trying to live up to that standard? _____

_____

_____

_____

_____

2. What are the benefits of keeping your virginity intact?

_____

_____

_____

_____

_____

3. What are the possible consequences for losing your virginity? _____

_____

_____

_____

_____

4. Why does God desire for you to take care of your body? In what ways can you do this? _____

_____

_____

_____

_____

5. Do you focus more on pleasing God or on pleasing people? Why?_____

_____

_____

_____

_____

Chapter 2
Telltale Signs

1. How easy is it for you to spot a virgin? List the ways in which you can tell a person is still a virgin. _____

_____

_____

_____

_____

2. How did Old Testament law punish women who were not virgins? What did they do to prove their virginity?

_____

_____

_____

_____

_____

3. What does the word *virginity* mean to you? How does it differ from the definition given in the chapter?

_____

_____

_____

_____

4. Do you believe it's possible to maintain virginity until marriage? Why or why not? _____

_____

_____

_____

_____

5. What is fornication, and why does it grieve God?

_____

_____

_____

_____

_____

Chapter 3

The Tokens of Virginity

1. What is a token?_____

_____

_____

_____

_____

_____

2. What seals a covenant relationship? Can this type of
relationship be broken?_____

_____

_____

_____

_____

3. List three tokens that prove you have accepted Christ as Lord and Savior. _____

_____

_____

_____

_____

_____

4. What three tokens protect your virginity? How?

_____

_____

_____

_____

_____

5. Why is it important to understand the value and purpose of these tokens? _____

_____

_____

_____

_____

Chapter 4

Purity

1. Is virginity a physical or mental state of being, or both? How are they linked together? _____

_____

_____

_____

_____

2. How did Satan deceive Adam and Eve in the Garden of Eden? _____

_____

_____

_____

_____

3. Do you believe impure thoughts lead to impure actions? Why, or why not? _____

_____

_____

_____

_____

_____

4. List your three favorite television shows. How do they portray sexual relationships? Does that image reflect the standards given in the Word of God?_____

_____

_____

_____

_____

5. What was it that led David—a man after God's own heart—to sin? What were the consequences of his actions?_____

_____

_____

_____

_____

Chapter 5

Innocence

1. What does it mean to be innocent in a court of law? What does it mean to be innocent as it relates to your virginity? _____

_____

_____

_____

_____

_____

2. In what way(s) does innocence protect your virginity?

_____

_____

_____

_____

_____

3. Matthew 10:16 commands us to be wise as serpents and innocent as doves. How difficult is this to do? Have you ever succeeded in doing so?_____

_____

_____

_____

_____

4. What does Satan attack first—your body or your mind? Why?_____

_____

_____

_____

5. What is the key to protecting your innocence?

_____

_____

_____

_____

_____

Chapter 6

The Blood

1. How is blood important to us physically? How is it
   important to us biblically?_____

   _____

   _____

   _____

   _____

2. What happens to the hymen during sexual intercourse?
   What does it signify?_____

   _____

   _____

   _____

   _____

3. How did Adam and Eve feel after they sinned? Why? What was God's reaction? _____

_____

_____

_____

_____

4. Why is it important to God that the marriage bed be kept pure? _____

_____

_____

_____

_____

5. Do you agree with the statement "Fornication is the final stage in the loss of your virginity"? Why, or why not?

_____

_____

_____

_____

_____

Chapter 7
Defending Your Castle

1. In the Middle Ages, what was the best way to capture a castle and the surrounding property? How did it work?

_____

_____

_____

_____

_____

2. How does Satan wage war against believers?

_____

_____

_____

_____

_____

3. What role does the Word of God play in defending your virginity?_____

_____

_____

_____

_____

4. What happens when one or more tokens have been damaged or are missing? _____

_____

_____

_____

_____

5. What is the key to your breakthrough?_____

_____

_____

_____

_____

_____

Chapter 8
A New Beginning

1. Think back over the past six months. Have you tried to overcome sexual temptation in your own strength? How?_____

_____

_____

_____

_____

_____

2. Read 1 John 1:9. What does this Scripture mean to you? How can you apply it to your own life?_____

_____

_____

_____

_____

3. How can the blood of Jesus renew your virginity?

_____

_____

_____

_____

_____

4. What is the difference between being a Christian and living like one? Which description applies to you?

_____

_____

_____

_____

_____

5. List at least three areas of your life that require more discipline. What will you do to bring about a permanent change in those areas?_____

_____

_____

_____

_____

Endnotes

Chapter 4

[1] *Merriam-Webster OnLine Dictionary,* copyright 2003, s.v. "subtle," available from <http://www.m-w.com>.

Chapter 8

[1] James Strong, *The New Strong's Complete Dictionary of Bible Words* (Nashville, Tennessee: Thomas Nelson Publishers, 1996), #4991, p. 706.

Prayer of Salvation

God loves you—no matter who you are, no matter what your past. God loves you so much that He gave His one and only begotten Son for you. The Bible tells us that "...whoever believes in him shall not perish but have eternal life" (John 3:16 NIV). Jesus laid down His life and rose again so that we could spend eternity with Him in heaven and experience His absolute best on earth. If you would like to receive Jesus into your life, say the following prayer out loud and mean it from your heart.

Heavenly Father, I come to You admitting that I am a sinner. Right now, I choose to turn away from sin, and I ask You to cleanse me of all unrighteousness. I believe that Your Son, Jesus, died on the cross to take away my sins. I also believe that He rose again from the dead so that I might be forgiven of my sins and made righteous through faith in Him. I call upon the name of Jesus Christ to be the Savior and Lord of my life. Jesus, I choose to follow You and ask that You fill me with the power of the Holy Spirit. I declare that right now I am a child of God. I am free from sin and full of the righteousness of God. I am saved in Jesus' name. Amen.

If you prayed this prayer to receive Jesus Christ as your Savior for the first time, please contact us on the web at www.harrisonhouse.com to receive a free book.

Or you may write to us at

Harrison House

P.O. Box 35035

Tulsa, Oklahoma 74153

About the Author

Carla A. Stephens hold an Associates degree in art from the Art Institute of Atlanta and graduated from the World Changers Church International (WCCI) School of Ministry in 1996 under the direction of Pastors Creflo and Taffi Dollar.

For the past eleven years she has counseled young men and women across the nation and shared the message of God's goodness and love. She serves in the youth ministry at World Changers Church International in College Park, Georgia, in addition to ministering in conferences, conventions, and workshops. She has served as the supervisor of Handmaidens of the Lord, an organization which trains and nurtures young women in their walk with God, and on the Women's Advisory Board alongside Pastor Taffi Dollar.

Carla firmly believes that no matter what challenges life may bring, they can always be overcome through prayer and with the Word of God.

Carla and her husband, Jesse, reside in the Atlanta, Georgia area with their son, Evan.

To contact Carla Stephens,

please write to:

Carla Stephens

P.O. Box 1630

Fayetteville, GA 30214

*Please include your prayer requests
and comments when you write.*

Additional copies of this book
are available from your local bookstore.

Harrison House
Tulsa, Oklahoma

If this book has been a blessing to you
or if you would like to see more of
the Harrison House product line,
please visit us on our website at
www.harrisonhouse.com.

The Harrison House Vision

Proclaiming the truth and the power
Of the Gospel of Jesus Christ
With excellence;

Challenging Christians to
Live victoriously,
Grow spiritually,
Know God intimately.